# The Book of **Bob**

# The Book of

# BOB

# Choice Words
# **Memorable Men**

Edited by Tom Crisp

**Andrews McMeel
Publishing, LLC**

Kansas City

09 10 11 RR2 10 9 8 7 6 5 4 3

Library of Congress Cataloging-in-Publication Data
The book of Bob : choice words, memorable men / edited by Tom Crisp.
    p. cm.
  ISBN-13: 978-0-7407-6365-6
  ISBN-10: 0-7407-6365-2
  1. Men—Quotations. 2. Quotations, American. 3. Quotations, English.
 I. Crisp, Tom.

PN6081.45.B66 2007
305.31—dc22

2006047207

Book design by Holly Camerlinck

www.andrewsmcmeel.com

**Attention: Schools and Businesses**
Andrews McMeel books are available at quantity discounts with bulk purchase for educational, business, or sales promotional use. For information, please write to: Special Sales Department, Andrews McMeel Publishing, LLC, 1130 Walnut Street, Kansas City, Missouri 64106

For

**Robert E. Lee Crisp,**

the most important Bob I'll ever know

# CONTENTS

# INTRODUCTION

**N**o name conjures up the everyman like the name Bob. Yessireebob, it is a *guy's* name. At the same time, "Robert" is an auspicious banner for any man to carry into life. It means *bright fame*, from the early German *hrod*, for "fame," and *beraht*, for "bright." Most Bobs will agree that the bright variety of fame is preferable to the dark, notorious kind. Comedian Bob Smith says, "Bob is short for Beelzebub," but that link is not firmly established.

More likely is a relation to the French *roi* for "king." And indeed, kings, saints, and rogues have had over a thousand years to write a legacy of *Roberthood*. (Not to be confused with Robin Hood—though his is one of the many variations of the name.)

Robert, or a version of it, is a popular name almost everywhere in the Western world, though nowhere as much as in the United States, where it ranks third among the male population. About thirty-four of every one thousand American men are called Bob, Bobby, Robert, or Rob. *Roberto* can be Italian, Spanish, or Portuguese. The Dutch and Germans call him *Rupert*, a name picked up by some of their cousin Brits. Finns say *Roopertti*, or *Roope* for short. *Robi* is Hungarian, while Bretons say *Roparzh*.

Whatever the accent, Robert is a grand old name that belongs to men with a great record of achievement, fame, and infamy. This book reveals something about them, but it is mostly things said—and written—*by* them: brilliant, bombastic, beneficent Bobbisms.

The surest way
to make a monkey
of a man
is to quote him.

**_Robert Benchley_**

# one

# To Know Him Is to
# Love Him

**A** great catch is like watching girls go by, the last one you see is always the prettiest.

> **Bob Gibson,** 1935–
> baseball player

**P**eople who throw kisses are hopelessly lazy.

> **Bob Hope,** 1903–2003
> comedian

If I were a girl, I'd despair. The supply of good women far exceeds that of the men who deserve them.

**Robert Graves,** 1895–1985
writer

They're the most wonderful, beautiful things put on this earth, and I'm not just saying that because they completely control and dominate my every breath.

**Bob Saget,** 1956–
actor/comedian

To my loving and lovely wife Veronica, who has unfailingly provided me with emotional, intellectual, spiritual, and controlled carbohydrate nourishment. *—book dedication*

**Robert Atkins, MD,** 1930–2003
diet authority

Older women are like aging strudels—the crust may not be so lovely, but the filling has come at last into its own.

**Robert Farrar Capon,** 1925–
writer/clergyman

Your hair's going to turn gray and fall out, you're going to get fat. You've got to experience those losses without getting bitter, without turning against the world. Unless you have the renewing power of falling in love available to you, life is very hard.

**Bob Kerrey,** 1943–
governor/U.S. senator, Nebraska/
president, New School University

Perhaps it is shameless to be so unabashedly romantic as to program "Body and Soul" immediately upon the heels of "Say It Isn't So," but such excesses are normal procedure when the lights are low and the wine is right.

**Bobby Short,** 1924–2005
singer/musician

**W**hy don't you step out of those wet clothes and into a dry martini?

> **Robert Benchley,** 1889–1945
> humorist

**S**ex without love is merely healthy exercise.

> **Robert A. Heinlein,** 1907–1988
> writer

**P**eople who can't think of anything else but whether the person you love is indented or convex should be doomed not to think of anything else but that, and so miss the other 95 percent of life.

> **Robert Towne,** 1934–
> actor/filmmaker

**G**ive me a kiss, and to that kiss a score;
Then to that twenty, add a hundred more:
A thousand to that hundred: so kiss on,
To make that thousand up a million.
Treble that million, and when that is done,
Let's kiss afresh, as when we first begun.   —*"To Anthea: Ah, My Anthea!"*

> **Robert Herrick,** 1591–1674
> poet

**L**ove can be understood only "from the inside," as a language can be understood only by someone who speaks it, as a world can be understood only by someone who lives in it.

> **Robert C. Solomon,** 1942–
> economist/educator

**"L**ove Makes the World Go 'Round"

—*song title from Broadway show* Carnival

> **Bob Merrill,** 1921–1998
> lyricist

**N**ever the time and the place and the loved one all together!

—*"Never the Time and the Place"*

> **Robert Browning,** 1812–1889
> poet

**W**omen often weep at weddings, whereas my own instinct is to laugh uproariously and encourage the bride and groom with merry whoops. The sight of people getting married exhilarates me; I think that they are doing a fine thing, and I admire them for it.

> **Robertson Davies,** 1913–1995
> writer

**V**ery often the only thing that comes between a charming man and a charming woman is the fact that they are married to each other.

—*with Gaston de Caillavet*

> **Robert de Flers,** 1872–1927
> writer/dramatist

**T**he memory of love is a powerful thing; it's a tangible possession in and of itself.

**Bob Seger,** 1945–
singer/songwriter

**D**on't get married to an actress, because they're also actresses in bed.

**Roberto Rossellini,** 1906–1977
filmmaker

**I**t's a funny thing that when a man hasn't anything on earth to worry about, he goes off and gets married.

**Robert Frost,** 1874–1963
poet

In every marriage more than a week old, there are grounds for divorce. The trick is to find, and continue to find, grounds for marriage.

**Robert Anderson,** 1917–
dramatist

All guys think I look like somebody who was in the service with them, and all women think I look like their first husband.

**Bob Newhart,** 1929–
comedian

I had a patient once who dreamed she kept her husband in the deep freeze except for mating. Lots of men feel that way.

**Robert A. Johnson,** 1921–
psychologist

**I**f we take matrimony at its lowest, we regard it as a sort of friendship recognized by the police.

> **Robert Louis Stevenson,**
> 1850–1894
> writer

**I**'ve got about sixteen more horses than I've had wives.

> **Bob Wills,** 1905–1975
> songwriter/bandleader
> (The Texas Playboys)

**I** was a multimillionaire from playing hockey. Then I got divorced, and now I am a millionaire.

> **Bobby Hull,** 1939–
> hockey player

**S**he got a mortgage on my body, now, and a lien on my soul.

—*"Traveling Riverside Blues"*

> **Robert Johnson,** 1911–1938
> musician/songwriter

**W**hen I was a boy, just old enough to be starting to date in a fumbling way, I complained something about girls. And my father said to me, "Would you rather hunt leopards or would you rather hunt rabbits? Which is going to be more fun?" And I decided I'd rather hunt leopards.

> **Robert Jordan,** 1948–
> writer

**L**ove is an irresistible desire to be irresistibly desired.

> **Robert Frost,** 1874–1963
> poet

**T**he plural of spouse is spice.

> **Robert Morley,** 1908–1992
> actor

**U**nto us all our days are love's anniversaries, each one
In turn hath ripen'd something of our happiness. *—"Anniversary"*

> **Robert Bridges,** 1844–1930
> poet

**A** man's family sets him apart from all other living creatures . . .
Only man stands with his children from first to last, from birth to
death, and to the grave.

> **Robert Nathan,** 1894–1985
> writer

**I**t's a wise child that knows its own father, but it's one child in a million who knows his own mother. They're a mysterious mob, mothers.

**Robertson Davies,** 1913–1995
writer

**I**f you're mad at your kid, you can either raise him to be a nose tackle or send him out to play on the freeway. It's about the same.

**Bob Golic,** 1957–
football player

**I** always liked kids. You can't kid a kid. They know right away if you like them or not.

**"Buffalo" Bob Smith,**
1917–1998
television host
*The Howdy Doody Show*

**W**hy do I have to be an example for your kid? You be an example for your own kid.

> **Bob Gibson,** 1935–
> baseball player

**T**he umpire has the awesome power
To send a grown man to the shower,
Yet cannot, in the aftermath,
Coerce his kids to take a bath.

—*"The Umpire"*

> **Bob McKenty,** 1935–
> poet

**I**f children and books truly expressed the unspoken desires of their creators, they'd all be named *Great Expectations*.

—Openly Bob

> **Bob Smith,** 1958–
> comedian/writer

**A**cross the years he could recall
His father one way best of all.
In the stillest hour of night
The boy awakened to a light.
Half in dreams, he was his sire
With his great hands full of fire.
The man had struck a match to see
If his son slept peacefully.

—*"The Secret Heart"*

> **Robert Tristram Coffin,**
> 1892–1955
> poet

**D**uty . . . is the sublimest word in our language. Do your duty in all things . . . You cannot do more—you should never wish to do less.

—*from a letter to his son*

> **Robert E. Lee,** 1807–1870
> U.S. military leader/general in chief of the Confederacy

**M**y songs are like my children: some you want around and some you want to send off to college as soon as possible.

**Bobby McFerrin,** 1950–
vocalist/conductor

**M**any children the world over have revealed a kind of toughness and plasticity that make the determined efforts of some parents to spare their children the slightest pain seem ironic.

**Robert Coles, MD,** 1929–
psychiatrist

**D**on't worry that children never listen to you; worry that they are always watching you.

**Robert Fulghum,** 1937–
writer/clergyman

**K**ids today are looking for idols, but sometimes they look too far . . . They don't have to look any farther than their home because those are the people that love you. They are the real heroes.

> **Bobby Bonilla,** 1963–
> baseball player

**L**ife was a lot simpler when what we honored was father and mother rather than all major credit cards.

> **Robert Orben,** 1927–
> humorist

**P**arents can plant magic in a child's mind through certain words spoken with some thrilling quality of voice, some uplift of the heart and spirit.

> **Robert MacNeil,** 1931–
> television journalist/writer

**T**he two most important things in life are good friends and a strong bullpen.

| **Bob Lemon,** 1920–2000
| baseball player

**F**riendship will not stand the strain of very much good advice for very long.

| **Robert Lynd,** 1879–1970
| sociologist

**S**o long as we love we serve; so long as we are loved by others, I would almost say that we are indispensable; and no man is useless while he has a friend.

| **Robert Louis Stevenson,**
| 1850–1894
| writer

For auld lang syne, my dear,
For auld lang syne,
We'll take a cup o' kindness yet
For auld lang syne!

—*"Auld Lang Syne"*

**Robert Burns,** 1759–1796
poet

# Rising to the Occasion

**O**hio physician Robert Holbrook Smith (Dr. Bob) was a miserable fifty-six-year-old drunk who had tried everything to quit the sauce. Then he met Bill Wilson (Bill W.), a recovering alcoholic himself. With Wilson's help, Smith finally succeeded, and in 1935 the two of them founded Alcoholics Anonymous.

By 1940 AA had a membership of about two thousand. Today there are more than two *million* members in 150 countries. Bill W. credited Dr. Bob with personally helping more than five thousand people achieve sobriety. Dr. Bob may have been one of the greatest friends of all time to people who didn't even know his last name.

# two

# Bobs of All Trades

If a man loves the labor of his trade, apart from any question of success or fame, the gods have called him.

**Robert Louis Stevenson,**
1850–1894
writer

You drive for show but putt for dough.

**Bobby Locke,** 1920–1987
golfer

**I** don't pay good wages because I have a lot of money; I have a lot of money because I pay good wages.

> **Robert Bosch,** 1861–1942
> industrialist

**T**he brain is a wonderful organ; it starts working the moment you get up in the morning and does not stop until you get into the office.

> **Robert Frost,** 1874–1963
> poet

**E**very day I get up and look through the *Forbes* list of the richest people in America. If I'm not there, I go to work.

> **Robert Orben,** 1927–
> humorist

There is so much bad news that I sometimes think we ought to start our newscast by saying, "I hate to tell you this, but . . ."

**Bob Schieffer,** 1937–
television journalist

Finance is the art of passing currency from hand to hand until it finally disappears.

**Robert W. Sarnoff,** 1918–
media executive

If I can't play for big money, I play for a little money. And if I can't play for a little money, I stay in bed that day.

**Bobby Riggs,** 1918–1995
tennis player

**W**hen you're doing what you love to do, the money comes naturally. Maybe not at first, but eventually . . . if you stick with it. Do you think Bob Hope started out with a goal, "I want to become a millionaire by making people laugh, then I'll retire to do what I want?" I doubt it. He just did what he did best. And the money came.

**Robert G. Allen,** 1948–
wealth guru


**G**et to know two things about a man. How he earns his money and how he spends it. You will then have the clue to his character. You will have a searchlight that shows up the inmost recesses of his soul. You know all you need to know about his standards, his motives, his driving desires, his real religion.

**Robert J. McCracken,** 1904–1973
clergyman

**W**hen I first heard Elvis's voice, I knew that I wasn't going to work for anybody . . . hearing him for the first time was like busting out of jail.

> **Bob Dylan,** 1941–
> singer/songwriter

**B**eing a star is an agent's dream, not an actor's.

> **Robert Duvall,** 1931–
> actor

**T**o be able to write a play a man must be sensitive, imaginative, naive, gullible, passionate; he must be something of an imbecile, something of a poet, something of a liar, something of a damn fool.

> **Robert E. Sherwood,** 1896–1955
> dramatist

We've all heard that a million monkeys banging on a million typewriters will eventually reproduce the complete works of Shakespeare. Now, thanks to the Internet, we know this is not true.

**Robert Wilensky,** 1951–
computer scientist

When you see something that is technically sweet, you go ahead and do it and you argue about what to do about it only after you have had your technical success.

**J. Robert Oppenheimer,**
1904–1967
physicist

I've not been cursed with talent, which could be a great inhibitor.

**Robert Rauschenberg,** 1925 –
artist

It often happens that when a person possesses a particular ability to an extraordinary degree, nature makes up for it by leaving him or her incompetent in every other department.

> **Robert Shea,** 1933–1994
> writer

I remember in the circus learning that the clown was prince, the high prince. I always thought the high prince was the lion or the magician, but the clown is the most important.

> **Roberto Benigni,** 1952–
> actor/filmmaker

Story is not only our most prolific art form but rivals all activities—work, play, eating, exercise—for our waking hours. We tell and take in stories as much as we sleep—and even then we dream.

> **Robert McKee,** 1941–
> screenwriter/lecturer

**T**he first flight with a rocket using liquid propellants was made yesterday at Aunt Effie's farm in Auburn. The day was clear and comparatively quiet.

*—journal entry (1926)*

**Robert H. Goddard,** 1882–1945
rocket scientist

**M**ake visible what, without you, might perhaps never have been seen.

**Robert Bresson,** 1907–1999
filmmaker

**O**ur responsibility as artists is to ask questions, that is to say *what is it* and not *what it is.* For if we know what it is we are doing there is no need to do it.

**Robert Wilson,** 1941–
dramatist/stage director

**I** want to be a story told round the world.

> **Robert Mapplethorpe,** 1946–1989
> photographer

**T**he bigger they are, the further they have to fall.

> **Bob Fitzsimmons,** 1863–1917
> world champion middleweight,
> heavyweight, and light
> heavyweight boxer

**I**n the old days they, the promoters, wanted more and more from me. They wanted me to jump or spill my blood and break my bones. Every time they wanted me to jump further, and further, and further. Hell, they thought my bike had wings.

> **Robert "Evel" Knievel,** 1938–
> daredevil/stuntman

**R**ed ice sells hockey tickets.

> **Bob Stewart,** 1950–
> hockey player

**O**ne good thing about music, when it hits you, you feel no pain.

> **Bob Marley,** 1945–1981
> musician/songwriter

**M**usic should never be harmless.

> **Robbie Robertson,** 1944–
> musician/songwriter (The Band)

**P**eople compose for many reasons: to become immortal; because the pianoforte happens to be open; because they want to become a millionaire; because of the praise of friends; because they have looked into a pair of beautiful eyes; for no reason whatsoever.

> **Robert Schumann,** 1810–1856
> composer/critic

**O**ne gets tired of the role critics are supposed to have in this culture: It's like being the piano player in a whorehouse; you don't have any control over the action going on upstairs.

**Robert Hughes,** 1938–
critic

**M**y mother—who was an alertly respectable woman—told me at an early age that I was not to play with critics.

**Robert Bolt,** 1924–1995
dramatist

**I**f the NBA were on Channel 5 and a bunch of frogs making love was on Channel 4, I'd watch the frogs even if they were coming in fuzzy.

**Bobby Knight,** 1940–
basketball coach

**I**f you take the game seriously, you go crazy anyway, so it helps if you're a bit nuts to start with because you don't waste time getting that way.

**Bob Plager,** 1943–
hockey player

**I** am trying—in a good cause—to crowd people out of their own minds and occupy their space. I want them to stop being themselves for the moment, I want them to stop thinking, and I want to occupy their heads.

**Robert Stone,** 1937–
writer

**A** director is a ringmaster, a psychiatrist, and a referee.

**Robert Aldrich,** 1918–1983
filmmaker

**I**t was a cross between a screwball and a change-up. It was a screw-up.

> **Robert Patterson,** 1959–
> baseball player

**M**ost people ignorantly suppose that artists are the decorators of our human existence, the esthetes to whom the cultivated may turn when the real business of the day is done . . . Far from being merely decorative, the artist's awareness is one of the few guardians of the inherent sanity and equilibrium of the human spirit that we have.

> **Robert Motherwell,** 1915–1991
> artist

**M**ost of the time I'm a professional idiot. I really don't care about what other people think, which can be a bad thing.

> **Robert Smith,** 1959–
> musician (The Cure)

**I** like the moment when I break a man's ego.

> **Bobby Fischer,** 1943–
> chess player

**A** man may be a tough, concentrated, successful money-maker and never contribute to his country anything more than a horrible example.

> **Robert G. Menzies,** 1894–1978
> prime minister, Australia

**P**erpetual devotion to what a man calls his business is only to be sustained by perpetual neglect of many other things.

> **Robert Louis Stevenson,**
> 1850–1894
> writer

If you have enough talent, you can write a story about a Danish prince if you've never been to Denmark, or war on the plains of Troy even if you're a blind man.

**Robert Morgan,** 1944–
writer

The average lawyer is essentially a mechanic who works with a pen instead of a ball peen hammer.

**Robert F. Schmitt,** 1934–
lawyer

Consultants are people who borrow your watch and tell you what time it is, and then walk off with the watch.

**Robert Townsend,** 1920–
business authority

"**M**y door is always open—bring me your problems." This is guaranteed to turn on every whiner, lackey, and neurotic on the property.

> **Robert F. Six,** 1907–1986
> president, Continental Airlines

**E**very man is dishonest who lives upon the labor of others, no matter if he occupies a throne.

> **Robert Green Ingersoll,**
> 1833–1899
> lawyer/politician/orator

**S**ome people tell me that we professional players are soccer slaves. Well, if this is slavery, give me a life sentence.

> **Bobby Charlton,** 1937–
> soccer player/manager

**A**ll good work is done in defiance of management.

| **Bob Woodward,** 1943–
| journalist

**B**y working faithfully eight hours a day you may eventually get to be boss and work twelve hours a day.

| **Robert Frost,** 1874–1963
| poet

**I** think my greatest proficiency is for showing up.

| **Bob Balaban,** 1945–
| actor/director

**A**nyone can do any amount of work provided it isn't the work he's supposed to be doing at the moment.

| **Robert Benchley,** 1889–1945
| humorist

**M**arket research can establish beyond the shadow of a doubt that the egg is a sad and sorry product and that it obviously will not continue to sell. Because after all, eggs won't stand up by themselves, they roll too easily, are too easily broken, require special packaging, look alike, are difficult to open, won't stack on the shelf.

> **Robert Pliskin,** 1917–
> graphic designer

**B**lack and white are the colors of photography. To me they symbolize the alternatives of hope and despair to which mankind is forever subjected.

> **Robert Frank,** 1924–
> photographer

**T**rying to describe something musical is like dancing to architecture.

> **Robert Palmer,** 1949–2003
> singer

**N**o matter how sublime your intuition as an artist might be, and how disciplined and acute your own cultivation of that intuition inside, your need for appreciation and recognition from the outside is crucial: as growing children need loving parents and supportive home and school environments, so do artists need their supporters.

**Robert Venturi,** 1925–
architect

**I** felt so painfully isolated that I vowed I would get revenge on the world by becoming a famous cartoonist.

**Robert Crumb,** 1943–
artist/illustrator

**F**rom the south side of Chicago, we thought going to California was like going to hell. So the day that I said, "I am going to U.S.C Film School," my father looked at me and said, "You're going to go join the circus?"

**Robert Zemeckis,** 1952–
filmmaker

**D**on't dance for the audience; dance for yourself.

> **Bob Fosse,** 1927–1987
> director/choreographer

**T**he mission of the playwright . . . is to look in his heart and write, to write whatever concerns him at the moment; to write with passion and conviction. Of course the measure of the man will be the measure of the play.

> **Robert Anderson,** 1917–
> dramatist

**T**he urge to write poetry is like having an itch. When the itch becomes annoying enough, you scratch it.

> **Robert Penn Warren,** 1905–1989
> writer

**T**o suggest is to create, to describe is to destroy.

> **Robert Doisneau,** 1912–1994
> photographer

**W**e take the shortest route to the puck and arrive in ill humor.

> **Bobby Clarke,** 1949–
> hockey player/manager

**W**hen I pick up the ball and it feels nice and light and small I know I'm going to have a good day. But if I pick it up and it's big and heavy, I know I'm liable to get into a little trouble.

> **Bob Feller,** 1918–
> baseball player

**M**athematics has given economics rigor, but alas, also mortis.

> **Robert Heilbroner,** 1919–2005
> economist

**W**hen a pianist sits down and does a virtuoso performance he is in a technical sense transmitting more information to a machine than any other human activity involving machinery allows.

> **Robert Moog,** 1934–
> sound engineer

**I**f your pictures aren't good enough, you aren't close enough.

> **Robert Capa,** 1913–1954
> photographer

**T**he invention of film has given our generation the dubious advantage of watching our acting heroes deteriorate before our eyes.

> **Robert Brustein,** 1927–
> educator/critic

**I** only wear the trench coat because I desperately want to be Robert Mitchum.

> **Robert Stack,** 1919–2003
> actor

**E**very two or three years I knock off for a while. That way I'm constantly the new girl in the whorehouse.

> **Robert Mitchum,** 1917–1997
> actor

**M**y vocal style I haven't tried to copy from anyone. It just developed until it became the girlish whine it is today.

**Robert Plant,** 1948–
singer (Led Zeppelin)

**M**y acting ability would have sent me back to the post office. It was my singing that got me jobs. Ironically, now, people think of me as an actor and don't know me much as a singer.

**Robert Guillaume,** 1927–
actor

**I** see my role as a successful businessman who applied for an NBA franchise, was able to write the check to get the franchise, and is now operating it like the other twenty-nine guys are operating their franchises.

—*on becoming the first black owner of an NBA team, the Charlotte Bobcats*

**Robert L. Johnson,** 1946–
media entrepreneur

**I**ndustry is not only the instrument of improvement, but the foundation of pleasure. He who is a stranger to it may possess, but cannot enjoy, for it is labor only which gives relish to pleasure.

**Robert Blair,** 1699–1746
poet

**D**elegating work works, provided the one delegating works, too.

**Robert Half,** 1918–
businessman

**W**ell, at the risk of being repetitious, we're gonna do another song in the key of D.

**Bob Weir,** 1947–
musician/singer
(The Grateful Dead)

**I** look upon myself as a musical bricklayer with architectural aspirations.

> **Robert Mayer,** 1879–1985
> philanthropist/founder of the
> London Philharmonic

**I**nterior design was invented when architects stopped making rooms that had character—when they said that a room was merely a box, a white walled cube.

> **Robert A. M. Stern,** 1939–
> architect

**I**'ll accept a commission from anyone who isn't frightened by my proposals.

> **Robert Denning,** 1935–
> interior designer

**I**f I'm meeting with somebody who is going to put the money up for the film, and he or she asks, "Is this going to have action in it?" "Oh, you bet. We're going to have lots of it, this is really going to be exciting." But what I mean by action and what they mean by action may be quite different.

> **Robert Altman,** 1925–2006
> filmmaker

**B**aseball hasn't been the national pastime for many years now—no sport is. The national pastime, like it or not, is watching television.

> **Bob Greene,** 1947–
> journalist

**I**'ve learned my song, and I sing it.

> **Bob Barker,** 1923–
> television host

**W**e can put a man on the moon, or build computers that can do virtually anything, but I submit that no technology can rival the technical complexity, paired with the transcendent beauty of the orchestra. The orchestra is essentially at the apex of human development, and truly represents the highest achievements of Western Civilization. Every instrument: its history, its pedagogy; every player, their years of commitment and individuality; the orchestral tradition and repertoire; and the alchemical combination of all of these, creating that amazing whole, the orchestra.

**Robert Aldridge,** 1954–
composer

**T**ake the time to write. You can do your life's work in half an hour a day.

**Robert Hass,** 1941–
poet

**P**oetry is no more a narcotic than a stimulant; it is a universal bittersweet mixture for all possible household emergencies and its action varies accordingly as it is taken in a wineglass or a tablespoon, inhaled, gargled, or rubbed on the chest by hard fingers covered with rings.

**Robert Graves,** 1895–1985
writer

**A**rt is an outsider, a gypsy over the face of the earth.

**Robert Henri,** 1865–1929
artist

**M**y thanks to the U.S. Navy. They taught me how to type.

**Robert Sward,** 1933–
writer

The deep sea is the biggest museum in the world . . . yet there's no lock on the door.

> **Robert Ballard,** 1945–
> oceanographer

Make no mistake: The weeds will win; nature bats last.

> **Robert M. Pyle,** 1947–
> naturalist/writer

Nothing flatters me more than to have it assumed that I could write prose—unless it be to have it assumed that I once pitched a baseball with distinction.

> **Robert Frost,** 1874–1963
> poet

**A**nybody with ability can play in the big leagues. But to be able to trick people year in and year out the way I did, I think that was a much greater feat.

> **Bob Uecker,** 1935–
> baseball player

**B**usy is the man with many hats and nothing to put them on.

> **Robert Priest,** 1951–
> writer

**I**'ve broken my nose this year and I put my teeth all the way through my lip. This is not good for my modeling career.

> **Robbie Paul,** 1976–
> rugby player

**A**thletes have other athletes as competitors. My competitor is death.

> **Robbie Knievel,** 1962–
> daredevil/stuntman

**B**y the end of the season I feel like a used car.

> **Bob Brenly,** 1954–
> baseball player/manager

**R**ule Number 1 is, don't sweat the small stuff. Rule Number 2 is, it's all small stuff. And if you can't fight and you can't flee, flow.

> **Robert S. Eliot, MD,** 1919–1996
> cardiologist

**I** write five pages a day. If you would read five pages a day, we'd stay right even.

> **Robert Parker,** 1932–
> writer

**I**t is just as important to be well danced as it is to be well versed or well read.

> **Robert Farris Thompson,** 1932–
> art historian

**T**his is a test. It is only a test. Had it been an actual job, you would have received raises, promotions, and other signs of appreciation.

> **Robert Benchley**, 1889–1945
> humorist

**M**aster, I've filled my contract, wrought in Thy many lands;
Not by my sins wilt Thou judge me, but by the work of my
    hands.
Master, I've done Thy bidding, and the light is low in the west,
And the long, long shift is over . . .
Master, I've earned it—
Rest.

*—"The Song of the Wage-Slave"*

> **Robert W. Service,** 1874–1958
> poet

# Being Bob

**S**o many men are given the name Robert that it's rare to discover a Bob who chose the name for himself. However, the most famous Bob of the twentieth century started out as a hoofer with a name that didn't suit his shtick.

Leslie Townes Hope had hit a plateau with his vaudeville act and decided to change his name to Bob. "It's chummier," Hope recalled. He claimed that his very next job—at $25 a show—paid him double what he was used to, and that soon he was earning ten times the amount. As Bob, Hope became the "world's most honored" entertainer, with five special Oscars, forty-four honorary degrees, the U.S. Medal of Freedom, and a knighthood, among dozens of other tributes.

For nearly sixty years Hope entertained U.S. troops in theaters of war—and peace—around the world. In 2003 President George W. Bush created the Bob Hope American Patriot Award to honor civilians who demonstrate that overwhelming regard for men and women in uniform.

# three

# Saints and Sinners, Losers and Winners

**P**rayer for many is like a foreign land. When we go there, we go as tourists. Like most tourists, we feel uncomfortable and out of place. Like most tourists, we therefore move on before too long and go somewhere else.

**Robert McAfee Brown,**
1920–2001
theologian/activist

The truth of the matter is that you always know the right thing to do. The hard part is doing it.

> **Robert H. Schuller,** 1926–
> clergyman

Example is more forcible than precept. People look at my six days in the week to see what I mean on the seventh.

> **Robert Gascoyne-Cecil,**
> **Lord Salisbury,** 1830–1903
> British foreign minister/three-time
> prime minister

The day that this country ceases to be free for irreligion, it will cease to be free for religion.

> **Robert H. Jackson,** 1892–1954
> U.S. attorney general/Supreme
> Court justice

**F**aith makes the discords of the present the harmonies of the future.

> **Robert Collyer,** 1823–1912
> clergyman

**T**o do what ought to be done but what would not have been done unless I did it, I thought to be my duty.

> **Robert Morrison,** 1782–1834
> missionary

**I**nasmuch as we Americans have grown up under the conditions of religious freedom, we often too easily forget that it came about only after centuries of struggle. Freedom in matters of religion was bought at a price—and for some courageous persons in the past, the cost was high.

> **Robert T. Handy,** 1918–
> historian

It is a truism that almost any sect, cult, or religion will legislate its creed into law if it acquires the political power to do so.

**Robert A. Heinlein,** 1907–1988
writer

In this enlightened age, there are few I believe, but what will acknowledge that slavery as an institution is a moral and political evil in any country.

**Robert E. Lee,** 1807–1870
U.S. military leader/general in chief of the Confederacy

In a world filled with hate, prejudice, and protest, I find that I too am filled with hate, prejudice, and protest.

**Bob Gibson,** 1935–
baseball player

**I** don't stand for the black man's side, I don't stand for the white man's side. I stand for God's side.

> **Bob Marley,** 1945–1981
> musician/songwriter

**M**y position was always the same, that race would not and should not be a part of this case. I was wrong. Not only did we play the race card, we dealt it from the bottom of the deck.

> *—on the O. J. Simpson trial and defense team*

> **Robert L. Shapiro,** 1942–
> lawyer

**Y**ou don't fight racism with racism, the best way to fight racism is with solidarity.

> **Bobby Seale,** 1936–
> activist/founder of the
> Black Panthers

**I** am the inferior of any man whose rights I trample under foot.

> **Robert Green Ingersoll,**
> 1833–1899
> lawyer/politician/orator

**S**top shallow water from running, it will rage; tread on a worm and it will turn.

> **Robert Greene,**
> sixteenth-century
> dramatist

**A**partheid is an insult to God and man whom God dignifies.

> **Robert Runcie,** 1921–2000
> archbishop of Canterbury

**C**oercion, after all, merely captures man. Freedom captivates him.

> **Robert S. McNamara,** 1916–
> U.S. secretary of defense

**P**eople say they love truth, but in reality they want to believe that which they love is true.

| **Robert Ringer,** 1938–
| writer

**T**ruth will lose its credit, if delivered by a person that has none.

| **Robert South,** 1634–1716
| clergyman

**I**t is a puzzling thing. The truth knocks on the door and you say, "Go away, I'm looking for the truth," and so it goes away. Puzzling.

| **Robert M. Pirsig,** 1928–
| philosopher

**C**onformity, humility, acceptance—with these coins we are to pay our fares to paradise.

| **Robert Lindner,** 1914–1956
| psychoanalyst

**A** long and wicked life followed by five minutes of perfect grace gets you into Heaven. An equally long life of decent living and good works followed by one outburst of taking the name of the Lord in vain—then have a heart attack at that moment and be damned for eternity. Is that the system?

**Robert A. Heinlein,** 1907–1988
writer

**Y**ou are only what you are when no one is looking.

**Robert C. Edwards,** 1914–
president, Clemson University

**Y**ou might as well praise a man for not robbing a bank.

*—on penalizing himself a stroke that cost him a championship*

**Bobby Jones,** 1902–1971
golfer

There is no more dangerous experiment than that of undertaking to be one thing before a man's face and another behind his back.

> **Robert E. Lee,** 1807–1870
> U.S. military leader/general in chief
> of the Confederacy

Forgive thyself little, and others much.

> **Robert Leighton,** 1611–1684
> clergyman/scholar

More people are flattered into virtue than bullied out of vice.

> **Robert Smith Surtees,**
> 1805–1894
> writer

People seldom do what they believe in. They do what is convenient, then repent.

> **Bob Dylan,** 1941–
> singer/songwriter

**F**aith . . . is confidence in what I have not seen but dearly hope to be the case.

> **Robert Hunter,** 1941–
> singer/songwriter/poet
> (The Grateful Dead)

**A**s the bomb fell over Hiroshima and exploded, we saw an entire city disappear. I wrote in my log the words: "My God, what have we done?"

> **Robert Lewis,** 1918–1983
> captain, U.S. Army Air Corps

**T**he Bible tells us to be like God, and then on page after page it describes God as a mass murderer. This may be the single most important key to the political behavior of Western Civilization.

> **Robert Anton Wilson,** 1932–
> philosopher

When you eat fish, you don't eat the bones. You eat the flesh. Take the Bible like that.

**Robert R. Moton,** 1867–1940
president, Tuskegee Institute

The priest is concerned with other people for the sake of God and with God for the sake of other people.

**Robert Runcie,** 1921–2000
archbishop of Canterbury

The nobility of England, my lord, would have snored through the Sermon on the Mount. —A Man for All Seasons

**Robert Bolt,** 1924–1995
dramatist

The preacher talks as on a phone where the line is dead.

**Robert Gorham Davis,**
1908–1998
educator

**D**emagoguery from the pulpit is no different from demagoguery on the campaign trail. If anything, it is worse, because it clothes itself in self-righteousness.

> **Robert B. Morgan,** 1925–
> U.S. senator, North Carolina

**I**n Genesis, seeing the world filled with violence, God decided to drown all mankind except Noah's family. But because that family carried the same genes as those who had drowned, violence continued unabated.

> **Robert Gorham Davis,**
> 1908–1998
> educator

**I**t is not the frequency of divorce which makes the times wicked; it is the wickedness of the times which increases divorce.

> **Robertson Davies,** 1913–1995
> writer

To have an ancestor who was hanged for sheep-stealing gives me a certain social standing, don't you think?

> **Robert Morley,** 1908–1992
> actor

You can jail a revolutionary but you cannot jail the revolution.

> **Bobby Seale,** 1936–
> activist/founder of the
> Black Panthers

Whenever men take the law into their own hands, the loser is the law. And when the law loses, freedom languishes.

> **Robert F. Kennedy,** 1925–1968
> U.S. attorney general/U.S. senator,
> New York

**I**t was so nice to go into this fake courtroom on *Ally McBeal*.
I immediately went up into the judge's chair. Nice view.
A preferable perspective.

> **Robert Downey Jr.,** 1965–
> actor


**I**t's such nonsense, this immorality of Hollywood. We're all too
tired.

> **Robert Lord,** 1900–1976
> filmmaker


**I**t's just like Palm Springs without the riffraff.

*—on jail time after conviction for marijuana possession*

> **Robert Mitchum,** 1917–1997
> actor

**I** don't think being a prostitute is any worse than being the head of a record company or a journalist.

> **Bobby Gillespie,** 1962–
> singer/songwriter (Primal Scream)

**W**hile we had a reputation as rampaging sexual vandals, the truth is that most of the time we were looking for nothing at bedtime other than a good paperback.

> **Robert Plant,** 1948–
> singer (Led Zeppelin)

**W**e don't want our players to be monks, we want them to be football players, because a monk doesn't play football at this level.

> **Bobby Robson,** 1933–
> soccer player/coach

**M**ost people would like to be delivered from temptation but would like it to keep in touch.

**Robert Orben,** 1927–
humorist

**L**iving with a saint is more grueling than being one.

**Robert Cummings Neville,**
1939–
philosopher

**T**o make our idea of morality center on forbidden acts is to defile the imagination and to introduce into our judgments of our fellow men a secret element of gusto.

**Robert Louis Stevenson,**
1850–1894
writer

**T**he world does not need tourists who ride by in a bus clucking their tongues. The world as it is needs those who will love it enough to change it, with what they have, where they are.

**Robert Fulghum,** 1937–
writer/clergyman

**I**f one by one we counted people out
For the least sin, it wouldn't take us long
To get so we had no one left to live with.
For to be social is to be forgiving.       —*"The Star Splitter"*

**Robert Frost,** 1874–1963
poet

**W**e cannot go about, unfortunately, telling everybody about the temptations we have resisted . . . people judge us exclusively by the temptations to which we yield.

**Robert Lynd,** 1879–1970
sociologist

**W**ittgenstein, Elizabeth Taylor, Bertrand Russell, Thomas Merton, Yogi Berra, Allen Ginsburg, Harry Wolfson, Thoreau, Casey Stengel, The Lubavitcher Rebbe, Picasso, Moses, Einstein, Hugh Hefner, Socrates, Henry Ford, Lenny Bruce, Baba Ram Dass, Gandhi, Sir Edmund Hillary, Raymond Lubitz, Buddha, Frank Sinatra, Columbus, Freud, Norman Mailer, Ayn Rand, Baron Rothschild, Ted Williams, Thomas Edison, H. L. Mencken, Thomas Jefferson, Ralph Ellison, Bobby Fischer, Emma Goldman, Peter Kropotkin, you, and your parents. Is there really one kind of life which is best for each of these people?

**Robert Nozick,** 1938–2002
philosopher

**I**t is my contention that most people are not mugged every day, that most people in this world do not encounter violence every day. I think we prepare people for violence, and I think just as importantly we prepare people for the definition of being gentle.

**Bob Keeshan** (aka Captain Kangaroo), 1927–2004
actor/producer

Let's not louse it all up with Freudian complexes and things that are interesting to the scientific mind, but have very little to do with our actual AA work. Our Twelve Steps, when simmered down to the last, resolve themselves into the words love and service. We understand what love is and we understand what service is.

**Robert Holbrook Smith, MD (Dr. Bob),** 1879–1950
cofounder, Alcoholics Anonymous

I am not an animal in my personal life. But in the ring there is an animal inside me. Sometimes it roars when the first bell rings. Sometimes it springs out later in a fight. But I can always feel it there, driving me and pushing me forward. It is what makes me win. It makes me enjoy fighting.

**Roberto Duran,** 1951–
boxer

**E**very winner has scars.

> **Robert N. C. Nix,** 1905–1987
> U.S. congressman, Pennsylvania

**A**lways keep your composure. You can't score from the penalty box; and to win, you have to score.

> **Bobby Hull,** 1939–
> hockey player

**I**f you think you've hit a false note, sing loud. When in doubt, sing loud.

> **Robert Merrill,** 1917–2004
> baritone

**G**ood pitching will beat good hitting any time, and vice versa.

> **Bob Veale,** 1935–
> baseball player

The success of *Bonnie and Clyde* made me very miserable. It's some deep-seated neurosis I have.

**Robert Benton,** 1932–
screenwriter

The greater the artist, the greater the doubt. Perfect confidence is granted to the less talented as a consolation prize.

**Robert Hughes,** 1938–
critic

The goal of discoverers is not to outdistance their peers but to transcend themselves. Hence individuals bent on real achievement should not waste too much of their time succeeding

**Robert Grudin,** 1938–
writer/educator

**I** am now Sitting Reduced to half a Crown, Without knowing Where to obtain a shilling for some months. This my Lord is an awkward sensation for a feeling Mind.

**Robert Fulton,** 1765–1815
inventor/engineer/artist

**A** minute's success pays the failure of years.

—*"Apollo and the Fates"*

**Robert Browning,** 1812–1889
poet

**H**appiness is not a reward—it is a consequence. Suffering is not a punishment—it is a result.

**Robert Green Ingersoll,**
1833–1899
lawyer/politician/orator

**I** had four or five hit records before "Mack the Knife" appealing to a younger set, that were rock and roll hits. And prior to that I had seven or eight failures that didn't appeal to anyone except my immediate family.

> **Bobby Darin,** 1936–1973
> singer

**I**f any of our songs ever did make it on the top ten, I'd disband the group immediately.

> **Robert Smith,** 1959–
> musician (The Cure)

**S**uccess is where preparation and opportunity meet.

> **Bobby Unser,** 1934–
> auto racing driver

**R**eal change is not made in taking the first step. It's made in the perpetual renewal of your commitment to change.

**Bob Greene,** 1963–
fitness trainer

**S**ooner or later everyone sits down to a banquet of consequences.

**Robert Louis Stevenson,**
1850–1894
writer

**I**'ll start shaving, I guess.

*—on how he planned to celebrate winning the Olympic decathlon at age seventeen*

**Bob Mathias,** 1930–2006
athlete/U.S. congressman, California

**T**o live only for some future goal is shallow. It's the sides of the mountain that sustain life, not the top

**Robert M. Pirsig,** 1928–
philosopher

**G**uts win more games than ability.

> **Bob Zuppke,** 1879–1957
> football coach

**I**'m really happy for Coach Cooper and the guys who've been around here for six or seven years, especially our seniors.

*—after winning a Big Ten title for Ohio State*

> **Bob Hoying,** 1972–
> football player

**P**laying safe is probably the most unsafe thing in the world. You cannot stand still. You must go forward.

> **Robert Collier,** 1855–1950
> marketing pioneer/writer

**O**ur business in life is not to succeed, but to continue to fail in good spirits.

> **Robert Louis Stevenson,**
> 1850–1894
> writer

**T**he good news is that our defense is giving up only one touchdown a game. The bad news is that our offense is doing the same.

> **Bobby Bowden,** 1929–
> football coach

**T**he man who can smile when things go wrong has thought of someone else he can blame it on.

> **Robert Bloch,** 1917–1994
> writer

**W**hen you blame others, you give up your power to change.

**Robert Anthony,** 1916–
writer

**A**s I've grown older, I've had to reconsider my dismissal of the story of Adam and Eve and the idea of original sin. Making one mistake and having it become a constant source of punishment and misery, retold over and over from one generation to the next, is a tradition of human nature that my family has always celebrated.

—Openly Bob

**Bob Smith,** 1958–
comedian/writer

**T**here is no limit to what a man can do or where he can go if he doesn't mind who gets the credit.

**Robert W. Woodruff,** 1889–1985
businessman

**F**orget about style; worry about results.

> **Bobby Orr,** 1948–
> hockey player

**D**on't think of it as failure. Think of it as time-released success.

> **Robert Orben,** 1927–
> humorist

**H**ow can a guy win a game if you don't give him any runs?

*—after losing a game 15–0*

> **Robert "Bo" Belinsky,**
> 1936–2001
> baseball player

**T**he key is not the "will to win" . . . everybody has that. It is the will to prepare to win that is important.

> **Bobby Knight,** 1940–
> basketball coach

**I**f it happens too often, losing leads to self-loathing, despair, and frightening eruptions of bile. I've heard of extreme cases where players got so sick and tired of losing at pool that they sank to bowling.

**Robert Byrne,** 1930–
writer/billiards authority

**M**ediocre teams are everywhere, but to be awful in a league of your own does carry a certain distinction. There's this huge difference between 0–16 and 2–14.

**Bob Verdi,** 1945–
journalist

**I**f history is written by the winners, it is won by the most ambitious.

**Robert Reich,** 1946–
U.S. secretary of labor/economist

**I** think I can do things I know I can't do.

> **Bob Keeshan** (aka Captain Kangaroo), 1927–2004
> actor/producer

**S**low and steady wins the race. —*"The Hare and the Tortoise"*

> **Robert Lloyd,** 1733–1764
> poet

**H**ard work without talent is a shame, but talent without hard work is a tragedy.

> **Robert Half,** 1918–
> businessman

**A** work of art is the trace of a magnificent struggle.

> **Robert Henri,** 1865–1929
> artist

If you are lucky enough to be a success, by all means enjoy the applause and the adulation of the public. But never, never believe it.

**Robert Montgomery,** 1904–1981
actor

You never become a howling success by just howling.

**Bob Harrington,** 1950–1992
theater critic/social worker

I was in the right place at the right time. Of course I steered myself there.

**Bob Hope,** 1903–2003
comedian

Living in a small town in Texas ain't half bad—if you own it.

**Bobby Layne,** 1926–1986
football player

**T**hey gave me star treatment because I was making a lot of money. But I was just as good when I was poor.

> **Bob Marley,** 1945–1981
> musician/songwriter

**A**las! Old man, we're wealthy now,
    it's sad beyond a doubt;
We cannot dodge prosperity,
    success has found us out.
Your eye is very dull and drear,
    my brow is creased with care,
We realize how hard it is
    to be a millionaire.

*—"The Joy of Being Poor"*

> **Robert W. Service,** 1874–1958
> poet

# Swear on a Stack of Bobs

**T**welve Roberts have been elevated to sainthood, most notably the brilliant and controversial Saint Robert Bellarmine (Italy, 1542–1621), cardinal, theologian, inquisitor, and doctor of the Roman Catholic Church. Over a period of tremendous volatility in the church, dealing with figures ranging from James I of England to Galileo, Robert Bellarmine remained an intellectual force to be reckoned with at the Vatican.

There has been no "Pope Robert." But philosopher and writer Robert Anton Wilson, coauthor with Robert Shea of the cult favorite *Illuminatus!* trilogy, is known as "Pope Bob" to many of his apostles.

# four

# A Man Among Men

There must be no barriers for freedom of inquiry. There is no place for dogma in science. The scientist is free, and must be free to ask any question, to doubt any assertion, to seek for any evidence, to correct any errors.

**J. Robert Oppenheimer,**
1904–1967
physicist

**W**e must accept life for what it actually is—a challenge to our quality without which we should never know of what stuff we are made, or grow to our full stature.

**Robert Louis Stevenson,**
1850–1894
writer

**G**enius not only diagnoses the situation but supplies the answers.

**Robert Graves,** 1895–1985
writer

**O**ne could write a history of science in reverse by assembling the solemn pronouncements of highest authority about what could not be done and could never happen.

**Robert A. Heinlein,** 1907–1988
writer

**E**very man of genius is considerably helped by being dead.

> **Robert Lynd,** 1879–1970
> sociologist

**A** tree growing out of the ground is as wonderful today as it ever was. It does not need to adopt new and startling methods.

> **Robert Henri,** 1865–1929
> artist

**I** happen to think that computers are the most important thing to happen to musicians since the invention of catgut, which was a long time ago.

> **Robert Moog,** 1934–
> sound engineer/inventor

**W**e get lost in a fog of abstraction and easily forget that man is a bloodhound sniffing for the real.

> **Robert C. Pollock,** 1901–1978
> philosopher

**S**urely there is grandeur in knowing that in the realm of thought, at least, you are without a chain; that you have the right to explore all heights and depth; that there are no walls nor fences, nor prohibited places, nor sacred corners in all the vast expanse of thought.

**Robert Green Ingersoll,**
1833–1899
lawyer/politician/orator

**E**very vision is a joke until the first man accomplishes it; once realized, it becomes commonplace.

**Robert H. Goddard,** 1882–1945
rocket scientist

**A** picture is not a canvas on the wall, it is the impact that hits the bull's-eye of your mind.

**Roberto Matta,** 1911–2002
artist

It is not so important to be serious as it is to be serious about the important things. The monkey wears an expression of seriousness which would do credit to any college student, but the monkey is serious because he itches.

**Robert M. Hutchins,** 1899–1977
president, University of
Chicago/editor


Don't give me any money, don't give me any people, but give me freedom, and I'll give you a movie that looks gigantic.

**Robert Rodriguez,** 1968–
film director


Ingenuity, plus courage, plus work, equals miracles.

**Bob Richards,** 1926–
pole-vaulter/clergyman

**C**reative achievement is the boldest initiative of the mind, an adventure that takes its hero simultaneously to the rim of knowledge and the limits of propriety. Its pleasure is not the comfort of the safe harbor, but the thrill of the reaching sail.

**Robert Grudin,** 1938–
writer/educator


**A**ll of us learn to write in the second grade. Most of us go on to greater things.

**Bobby Knight,** 1940–
basketball coach


**I** was full of pie, ice cream, and inexperience. To me, golf was just a game to beat someone. I didn't know that someone was me.

**Bobby Jones,** 1902–1971
golfer

**R**ecords which inspire people—whether it be to hate the music or to love it—are the only kinds of records to make.

**Rob Dickinson,** 1965–
songwriter/musician
(Catherine Wheel)

**A**n odd contradiction, if the layman were correct in his unconscious assumption that the artist begins with reality and ends with art: The converse is true—to the degree that this dichotomy has any truth—the artist begins with art, and through it arrives at reality.

**Robert Motherwell,** 1915–1991
artist

**W**hen you do not know what you are doing and what you are doing is the best—that is inspiration.

**Robert Bresson,** 1907–1999
filmmaker

**I** do not "get" ideas; ideas get me.

> **Robertson Davies,** 1913–1995
> writer

**L**ook for opportunity, not guarantees.

> **Robert Anthony,** 1916–
> writer

**G**oals must never be from your ego, but problems that cry for a solution.

> **Robert H. Schuller,** 1926–
> clergyman

**I**f well thou hast begun, go on foreright;
It is the end that crowns us, not the fight.  —*"The End"*

> **Robert Herrick,** 1591–1674
> poet

**I**t has often proved true that the dream of yesterday is the hope of today, and the reality of tomorrow. *—high school oration*

**Robert H. Goddard,** 1882–1945
rocket scientist

**T**hat four great nations, flushed with victory and stung with injury, stay the hand of vengeance and voluntarily submit their captive enemies to the judgment of the law is one of the most significant tributes that Power has ever paid to Reason.

*—opening address to the military tribunal at Nuremberg, Germany, 1945*

**Robert H. Jackson,** 1892–1954
U.S. attorney general/Supreme
Court justice

**P**eace is not something you wish for; it's something you make, something you do, something you are, and something you give away.

**Robert Fulghum,** 1937–
writer/clergyman

**C**ourage without conscience is a wild beast.

> **Robert Green Ingersoll,**
> 1833–1899
> lawyer/politician/orator

**I** created Bruce Wayne to be a normal human being living in our society. I didn't want a second Superman. Every human being can relate to being a Batman.

> **Bob Kane,** 1915–1998
> comic book artist/writer

**P**rogress is a nice word. But change is its motivator. And change has its enemies.

> **Robert F. Kennedy,** 1925–1968
> U.S. attorney general/U.S. senator,
> New York

**M**oving fast is not the same as going somewhere.

> **Robert Anthony,** 1916–
> writer

**I**f the only new thing we have to offer is an improved version of the past, then today can only be inferior to yesterday. Hypnotized by images of the past, we risk losing all capacity for creative change.

> **Robert Hewison,** 1943–
> writer

**E**verything is in a state of flux, including the status quo.

> **Robert Byrne,** 1930–
> writer/billiards authority

**T**he boldest single marketing move in the history of the consumer goods business. *—introducing the ill-fated "New Coke"*

> **Roberto C. Goizueta,** 1931–1997
> chairman, Coca-Cola

**T**he best-laid schemes o' mice an' men
Gang aft agley.      *—"To a Mouse, on Turning Her Up in Her Nest with the Plow"*

> **Robert Burns,** 1758–1796
> poet

**C**hance is another name that we give to our mistakes. And all of the best things in my films are mistakes.

> **Robert Altman,** 1925–2006
> filmmaker

**L**eaders do not sway with the polls. Instead, they sway the polls through their own words and actions.

> **Robert L. Ehrlich,** 1957–
> governor, Maryland

**O**nce you sink in that first stake, they'll never make you pull it up.

> **Robert Moses,** 1888–1981
> city planning pioneer

**H**ard times don't create heroes. It is during the hard times when the "hero" within us is revealed.

**Bob Riley,** 1944–
U.S. congressman/governor,
Alabama

**H**ow can you expect an ordinary man to "understand and explain" any section of the Constitution, to correspond to the interpretation put upon it by the manager of election, when by a very recent decision of the Supreme Court, composed of the most learned men in the State, two of them put one construction upon a section, and the other justice put an entirely different construction upon it.

—*addressing the South Carolina Constitutional Convention of 1895 about disenfranchisement articles*

**Robert Smalls,** 1839–1916
former slave/Union ship captain/U.S. congressman, South Carolina

**I** shall find a way or make one.

> **Robert Edwin Peary,** 1856–1920
> rear admiral, U.S. Navy/North Pole
> explorer

**I** was lucky. My grandmother stepped up for me and said she would take responsibility for me and a compassionate juvenile judge took a chance and gave me one. They were getting ready to send me away to do real time, but they sent me instead to a juvenile alternative day school. And I guess that was the beginning of my turnaround.

> **Bob Beamon,** 1946–
> Olympic long jump champion

**A**ll of us might wish at times that we lived in a more tranquil world, but we don't. And if our times are difficult and perplexing, so are they challenging and filled with opportunity.

> **Robert F. Kennedy,** 1925–1968
> U.S. attorney general/U.S. senator,
> New York

**W**hen it becomes more difficult to suffer than to change . . . you will change.

> **Robert Anthony,** 1916–
> writer

**I** have brought you to the ring, now you must dance.

> —*to his troops at the battle of Bannockburn*

> **Robert I (Robert the Bruce),**
> 1274–1329
> king of Scotland

**I** will tell you privately it's not going to get better, it's going to get worse all the time, but don't fret. Remember, we "play the ball where it lies," and now let's not talk about this, ever again.

> **Bobby Jones,** 1902–1971
> golfer (diagnosed at age forty-six
> with syringomyelia, a spinal cord
> disorder)

**L**eaders are visionaries with a poorly developed sense of fear and no concept of the odds against them.

> **Robert Jarvik, MD,** 1946–
> inventor of the first permanent
> artificial heart

**I** may as well confess that I had no predilection for polar exploration.

> **Robert Falcon Scott,** 1868–1912
> British naval officer/South Pole
> expedition leader

**I**t was one thing to fly through the fury and hot steel of the German occupation forces in France and expect that at any moment you might get blown to smithereens. But what really turned my crank that day was the idea that I'd have to miss a hot date in London.

> **Robert Morgan,** 1918–2004
> colonel, U.S. Air Force/captain of
> the *Memphis Belle*

**F**ear is excitement without breath.

> **Robert Heller,** 1933–
> editor/management authority

**Y**ou notice that on all sides the instruments of destruction, the piling up of arms, is becoming greater; the instruments of death are more active and more numerous, and they are improved with every year; and each nation is bound for its own safety's sake to take part in this competition. The one hope that we have to prevent this competition from ending in a terrible effort of mutual destruction which will be fatal to Christian civilization—the only hope we have is that the Powers may gradually be brought together in a friendly spirit on all questions of difference which may arise, until at last they shall be welded in some international constitution which shall give to the world, as a result of their great strength, a long spell of unfettered and prosperous trade and continued peace. *—Nobel Peace Prize acceptance speech*

> **E. A. Robert Cecil,** 1864–1958
> British member of parliament/
> principal architect of the League
> of Nations

**I** don't want my epitaph on my gravestone to read, "He made a bunch of movies." Or even "He made good movies." As much as I love my art, I would like my life to have a value beyond my art, even if it's just a thought or a feeling in my son's mind.

**Robert Zemeckis,** 1952–
filmmaker

**A** good leader needs to have a compass in his head and a bar of steel in his heart.

**Robert Townsend,** 1920–
businessman

**I**f we were all determined to play the first violin we should never have an ensemble. Therefore, respect every musician in his proper place.

**Robert Schumann,** 1810–1856
composer/critic

**I**'m thirty-four years old and I'm still a boy having to prove myself over again every time out. But if I've spent my life playing a boy's game, it's still what I do. And because it's what I do, I want to be the best. It's not enough to be good enough. It's not enough to be very good. I have to be the best because that's what it's all about.

*—at his retirement*

**Bob Cousy,** 1928–
basketball player

**I**t is idleness that creates impossibilities; and where people don't care to do anything, they shelter themselves under a permission that it cannot be done.

**Robert South,** 1634–1716
clergyman

**M**en who were stronger, bigger, and faster than I was could have done it, but they never picked up a pole, and never made the feeble effort to pick their legs off the ground and get over the bar.

**Bob Richards,** 1926–
pole-vaulter/clergyman

**A** dwarf standing on the shoulders of a giant may see farther than a giant himself.

**Robert Burton,** 1577–1640
clergyman/scholar

**D**on't worry about humility. The easiest job God has to do is to keep you and me humble. God's biggest job is to get us to believe that we are somebody and that we really can do something.

**Robert H. Schuller,** 1926–
clergyman

**A**h, but a man's reach should exceed his grasp,
Or what's a heaven for?

—*"Andrea del Sarto"*

**Robert Browning,** 1812–1889
poet

# Overnight Success

**A** 1920 *New York Times* editorial said that Robert H. Goddard, now considered the "Father of Modern Rocketry," lacked "the knowledge ladled out daily in high schools." The newspaper referred to his publication of *A Method of Reaching Extreme Altitudes,* and scoffed at the notion of propulsion through the vacuum of space.

It wasn't until 1969—twenty-four years after Goddard's death—that the *Times* printed a retraction that coincided with man's first steps on the moon.

# five

# Patriot/Pundit/Politician/
# Philosopher

**I** like America, just as everybody else does. I love America, I gotta say that. But America will be judged.

**Bob Dylan,** 1941–
singer/songwriter

**A**uthority has every reason to fear the skeptic, for authority can rarely survive in the face of doubt.

**Robert Lindner,** 1914–1956
psychoanalyst

**A**merica's true power lies not in its will to dominate but in its ability to inspire.

> **Robert C. Byrd,** 1917–
> U.S. senator, West Virginia

**W**e love our native country, much as it has wronged us; and in the peaceable exercise of our inalienable rights, we will cling to it . . . Will you starve our patriotism?

> **Robert Purvis,** 1810–1898
> abolitionist

**S**lavery is but half abolished, emancipation is but half completed, while millions of freemen with votes in their hands are left without education.

> **Robert C. Winthrop,** 1809–1894
> U.S. congressman/senator,
> Massachusetts

**S**omething is wrong with America. I wonder sometimes what people are thinking about or if they're thinking at all.

> **Bob Dole,** 1923–
> U.S. senator, Kansas

**F**reedom to differ is not limited to things that do not matter much. That would be a mere shadow of freedom. The test of its substance is the right to differ as to things that touch the heart of the existing order.

> **Robert H. Jackson,** 1892–1954
> U.S. attorney general/Supreme
> Court justice

**V**irginia is my country, her I will obey, however lamentable the fate to which it may subject me.

> **Robert E. Lee,** 1807–1870
> U.S. military leader/general in chief
> of the Confederacy

**B**efore the war is ended, the war party assumes the divine right to denounce and silence all opposition to war as unpatriotic and cowardly.

> **Robert M. La Follette,**
> 1855–1925
> U.S. congressman/senator/
> governor, Wisconsin

**A**s a matter of general principle, I believe there can be no doubt that criticism in time of war is essential to the maintenance of any kind of democratic government.

> **Robert A. Taft,** 1889–1953
> U.S. senator, Ohio

**T**hey now ring the bells, but they will soon wring their hands.

> *—on the declaration of war against Spain, 1739*

> **Robert Walpole,** 1676–1745
> first (de facto)
> British prime minister

**N**either conscience nor sanity itself suggests that the United States is, should, or could be the global gendarme.

> **Robert S. McNamara,** 1916–
> U.S. secretary of defense

**T**hose who dare to interpret God's will must never claim Him as an asset for one nation or group rather than another. War springs from the love and loyalty which should be offered to God being applied to some God substitute, one of the most dangerous being nationalism.

> **Robert Runcie,** 1921–2000
> archbishop of Canterbury

**Y**ears ago, in the days of the Greeks, wars were postponed to make room for the Olympic games. In modern times, the Games have been postponed twice—to make room for wars.

> **Bob Mathias,** 1930–2006
> athlete/U.S. congressman,
> California

**H**uman war has been the most successful of our cultural traditions.

> **Robert Ardrey,** 1908–1980
> anthropologist

**W**orld peace cannot be safeguarded without the making of creative efforts proportionate to the dangers which threaten it.

> **Robert Schuman,** 1886–1963
> French prime minister/foreign
> minister/first president of
> European Parliament

**T**here is no new, inexpensive, or magic way to win wars in the near future. We must be able to defend ourselves and to win battles with tested, available armaments . . . Any premature adoption of the most modern but untried weapons and devices could lead to possible disaster.

> **Robert A. Lovett,** 1895–1986
> U.S. secretary of defense

Tanks come in two forms: the dangerous, deadly kind and the "liberating" kind.

**Robert Fisk,** 1946–
journalist

War is like an aging actress: more and more dangerous and less and less photogenic.

**Robert Capa,** 1913–1954
photographer

The belief in the possibility of a short decisive war appears to be one of the most ancient and dangerous of human illusions.

**Robert Lynd,** 1879–1970
sociologist

It is well that war is so terrible—we shouldn't grow too fond of it.

**Robert E. Lee,** 1807–1870
U.S. military leader/general in chief
of the Confederacy

**T**he stone statues of the abstract Union Soldier
grow slimmer and younger each year—.           *—"For the Union Dead"*

> **Robert Lowell,** 1917–1977
> poet

**T**he American dream has always depended on the dialogue
between the present and the past. In our architecture, as in all
our other arts—indeed, as in our political and social culture as
a whole—ours has been a struggle to formulate and sustain a
usable past.

> **Robert A. M. Stern,** 1939–
> architect

**T**he whole country is one vast insane asylum and they're letting
the worst patients run the place.

> **Robert Welch,** 1899–1985
> businessman/founder,
> John Birch Society

**A**merica's one of the finest countries anyone ever stole.

> **Bob "Bobcat" Goldthwaite,** 1962–
> comedian

**E**very president needs an S.O.B. and I'm Nixon's.

> **H. R. "Bob" Haldeman,**
> 1926–1993
> politician/White House chief of staff

**I**f you're hanging around with nothing to do and the zoo is closed, come over to the Senate. You'll get the same kind of feeling and you won't have to pay.

> **Bob Dole,** 1923–
> U.S. senator, Kansas

**I**s it any wonder why the approval ratings of the Congress go up every time we go into recess?

> **Robert C. Byrd,** 1917–
> U.S. senator, West Virginia

*Interviewer (Bob):* . . . through your various administrations, you've managed to riddle each and every department with corruption, from the top all the way through even to the visiting nurse association . . . Do you think it's easier to be corrupt now than it was, say, ten or fifteen years ago?

*Mayor (Ray):* Oh, my, yes! Ten or fifteen years ago it was a disgrace to be corrupt. Now it's a rich, fertile field. I would recommend it to anyone with a devious mind, who is willing to put in long hours without working hard.

> **Bob Elliott** (1923– )
> with Ray Goulding (1922–1990)
> comedians

**A**braham Lincoln did not go to Gettysburg having commissioned a poll to find out what would sell in Gettysburg. There were no people with percentages for him, cautioning him about this group or that group or what they found in exit polls a year earlier. When will we have the courage of Lincoln?

> **Robert Coles, MD,** 1929–
> psychiatrist

**T**he truth is, I suspect I'm the only CIA officer to have had two secretaries of state, a secretary of defense, and the general secretary of the Soviet Communist Party all try at different times to get me fired—a dubious disinction that would have turned a lesser man's hair gray.

**Robert M. Gates,** 1943–
U.S. CIA director/president, Texas A&M University/U.S. secretary of defense

**I**s there really someone who, searching for a group of wise and sensitive persons to regulate him for his own good, would choose that group of people that constitute the membership of both houses of Congress?

**Robert Nozick,** 1938–2002
philosopher

**P**oetry is about the grief. Politics is about the grievance.

**Robert Frost,** 1874–1963
poet

**T**he tendency for politicians to claim credit for favorable news is as natural as flatulence in cows.

**Robert J. Samuelson,** 1945–
journalist

**I**llegal aliens have always been a problem in the United States. Ask any Indian.

**Robert Orben,** 1927–
humorist

**W**hile Europe's eye is fix'd on mighty things,
The fate of empires and the fall of kings;
While quacks of State must each produce his plan,
And even children lisp the Rights of Man;
Amid this mighty fuss just let me mention,
The Rights of Woman merit some attention.   —*"The Rights of Woman"*

**Robert Burns,** 1758–1796
poet

At least 3 percent of the signers of the Constitution must have been gay, since that's the low estimate for any population sample. It was probably higher, given that they were a pretty talented bunch and wore wigs.

**Robert Scheer,** 1936–
journalist

If you elect a matinee idol mayor, you're going to have a musical comedy administration.

**Robert Moses,** 1888–1981
city planning pioneer

Ronald Reagan is not a typical politician because he does not know how to lie, cheat, and steal. He's always had an agent for that.

**Bob Hope,** 1903–2003
comedian

**B**ut very often in politics we have the experience called up from my father when someone was trying to help him in the campaign: I can take care of my enemies, may the Good Lord save me from my friends.

**Bob Bennett,** 1933–
U.S. senator, Utah

**I**t is hard to write about politicians, see them at such close range, and still think of any of them as heroes.

**Robert Novak,** 1931–
journalist

**N**ewspapermen, as journalists used to be called, have long been charged with the sin of cynicism . . . a characterization that many of us encourage to deflect attention from our far more widespread flaw, incorrigible sentimentalism.

**Robert Manning,** 1943–
writer/editor

The real appeal of the *News*, I think, is that it lights up the narrow routine of millions of lives with gleams from the great outside. Its readers thrill with secondhand emotions they will never know, they shudder from crimes they will never commit, they quiver with courage that shall never be theirs.

**Robert Shand**
managing editor, the New York
*Daily News*

Call it vanity, call it arrogant presumption, call it what you wish, but I would grope for the nearest open grave if I had no newspaper to work for, no need to search for and sometimes find the winged word that just fits, no keen wonder over what each unfolding day may bring.

**Bob Considine,** 1906–1975
journalist/television host

**T**he media's like a big dinosaur with a tail that swings back and forth and it indiscriminately knocks things over, both good and bad, and that's the freedom of the press, so what are you going to do?

**Robert De Niro,** 1943–
actor

**O**ne way or another, artists can't help responding to current events. The question isn't whether, it's how—with denial always an option.

**Robert Christgau,** 1942–
journalist

**C**ricket civilizes people and creates good gentlemen. I want everyone to play cricket in Zimbabwe; I want ours to be a nation of gentlemen.

**Robert Mugabe,** 1924–
prime minister/president,
Zimbabwe

**S**ome president wishes to be reelected, and thereupon speaks about the Bible as "the cornerstone of American Liberty." This sentence is a mouth large enough to swallow any church, and from that time forward the religious people will be citing that remark of the politician to substantiate the inspiration of the Scriptures.

**Robert Green Ingersoll,**
1833–1899
lawyer/politician/orator

**P**eople driven by enmity or by a need to dominate will not respond to reason or goodwill. They will manipulate civilized rules for uncivilized ends.

**Robert Zoellick,** 1953–
U.S. trade representative/deputy secretary of state

There is always a danger that human beings will lose interest in liberty as soon as they have achieved it or—worse still perhaps—use their newfound liberty to destroy the liberty of others.

**Robert Lynd,** 1879–1970
sociologist

Never forget posterity when devising a policy. Never think of posterity when making a speech.

**Sir Robert G. Menzies,**
1894–1978
prime minister, Australia

The average politician goes through a sentence like a man exploring a disused mine shaft—blind, groping, timorous, and in imminent danger of cracking his shins on a subordinate clause or a nasty bit of subjunctive.

**Robertson Davies,** 1913–1995
writer

**E**very speaker has a mouth;
An arrangement rather neat.
Sometimes it's filled with wisdom.
Sometimes it's filled with feet.

> **Robert Orben,** 1927–
> humorist

**I**t is characteristic of all movements and crusades that the psychopathic element rises to the top.

> **Robert Lindner,** 1914–1956
> psychoanalyst

**Y**ou are never dedicated to something you have complete confidence in. When people are fanatically dedicated to political or religious faiths, or any other kind of dogmas or goals, it's always because these dogmas or goals are in doubt . . . No one is fanatically shouting that the sun is going to rise tomorrow. They know it's going to rise tomorrow.

> **Robert M. Pirsig,** 1928–
> philosopher

**W**hat's a cult? It just means not enough people to make a minority.

> **Robert Altman,** 1925–2006
> filmmaker

**T**he gun which produces the vote should remain its security officer—its guarantor.

> **Robert Mugabe,** 1924–
> prime minister/president,
> Zimbabwe

**D**isloyalty, however picayune, is unforgivable to the fanatic. Even the appearance of disloyalty is sufficient for banishment of the offender, no matter how many years of unquestioned devotion have been given; they are as nothing compared to the enormity of the moment.

> **Robert Nisbet,** 1913–1996
> sociologist

**W**hat is objectionable, what is dangerous about extremists, is not that they are extreme, but that they are intolerant. The evil is not what they say about their cause, but what they say about their opponents.

**Robert F. Kennedy,** 1925–1968
U.S. attorney general/U.S. senator,
New York

**W**e refuse to lie here in dishonor! We are not criminals, but Irishmen! This is the crime of which we stand accused.

**Bobby Sands,** 1954–1981
writer/activist

**I**f I had my way about it they'd all be sent back to Russia or some other unpleasant place.

—*testifying to the House Un-American Activities Committee, 1947, on communists in Hollywood*

**Robert Taylor,** 1911–1969
actor

**T**here is something wrong in a government where they who do the most have the least. There is something wrong when honesty wears a rag, and rascality a robe; when the loving, the tender, eat a crust, while the infamous sit at banquets.

**Robert Green Ingersoll,**
1833–1899
lawyer/politician/orator

**A**gitation is the marshalling of the conscience of a nation to mold its laws.

**Robert Peel,** 1788–1850
member of Parliament/British
home secretary/prime minister

**J**ustice should remove the bandage from her eyes long enough to distinguish between the vicious and the unfortunate.

**Robert Green Ingersoll,**
1833–1899
lawyer/politician/orator

**W**hen any government, or any church for that matter, undertakes to say to its subjects, this you may not read, this you must not see, this you are forbidden to know, the end result is tyranny and oppression no matter how holy the motives.

> **Robert A. Heinlein,** 1907–1988
> writer

**T**he best things and best people rise out of their separateness; I'm against a homogenized society because I want the cream to rise.

> **Robert Frost,** 1874–1963
> poet

**A** ship with a great deal of sail but a very shallow keel.

*—on Constitutional law*

> **Robert H. Bork,** 1927–
> legal scholar

**A**s long as there are only three to four people on the floor, the country is in good hands. It's only when you have fifty to sixty in the Senate that you want to be concerned.

> **Bob Dole,** 1923–
> U.S. senator, Kansas


**T**hat's what the Senate is about. It's the last bastion of minority rights, where a minority can be heard, where a minority can stand on its feet, one individual if necessary, and speak until he falls into the dust. *—on the filibuster*

> **Robert C. Byrd,** 1917–
> U.S. senator, West Virginia


**I**f you're not a Bob Dornan, you don't know your history, don't know your facts. Everyone should be a Bob Dornan.

> **Bob Dornan,** 1933–
> U.S. congressman, California

**I**'ve gone from Nebraska, where people thought I was a liberal, to New York, where people think I'm a right-wing nutcase.

> **Bob Kerrey,** 1943–
> governor/U.S. senator,
> Nebraska/president, New School
> University

**Y**ou really have to get to know Dewey to dislike him.

> **Robert A. Taft,** 1889–1953
> U.S. senator, Ohio

**H**e is the cutlery man of Australia. He was born with a silver spoon in his mouth, speaks with a forked tongue, and knifes his colleagues in the back. *—on predecessor Malcolm Fraser*

> **Bob Hawke,** 1929–
> prime minister, Australia

**T**o congratulate oneself on one's warm commitment to the environment, or to peace, or to the oppressed, and think no more is a profound moral fault.

**Robert Conquest,** 1917–
writer/historian

**I** think the environment should be put in the category of our national security. Defense of our resources is just as important as defense abroad. Otherwise what is there to defend?

**Robert Redford,** 1937–
actor/filmmaker

**A** man's identity is not best thought of as the way in which he is separated from his fellows but the way in which he is united with them.

**Robert Terwilliger,** 1917–1991
director, Trinity Institute

**N**ationalism leads to totalitarianism, and totalitarianism leads to idolatry. It becomes not a principle of politics but a new religion and, let me add, a false religion. It depends partly on a pseudoscientific doctrine of race which leads inevitably to the antithesis of all that we value in Christian morality.

*—Nobel Peace Prize acceptance speech*

> **E. A. Robert Cecil,** 1864–1958
> British member of Parliament/
> a principal architect of the
> League of Nations

**I** would rather have my fate in the hands of twenty-three representative citizens of the country than in the hands of a politically appointed judge.

*—on the grand jury*

> **Robert Morgenthau,** 1919–
> district attorney, New York City

**D**emocracy is the name we give to the people each time we need them.

**Robert de Flers,** 1872–1927
writer/dramatist


**P**ut not your trust in Kings and Princes:
Three of a kind will take them both.          *—Rules for Playing Poker*

**Robert C. Schenck,** 1809–1890
U.S. congressman, Ohio/diplomat

# Roberts Rule

**H**istory's first head of state "Bob," who ruled just a year, was Robert I of France (ca. 866–923), a grandson of Charlemagne. Though he didn't quite spawn a "Robertmania," his great-grandson Robert II (the Pious, 972–1031) may have helped do so: *His* granddaughter married William of Normandy, the son of one Robert I (the Magnificent), duke of Normandy. The groom was later to be known as William I (the Conqueror, ca. 1028–1087), who named his own first son Robert (Curthose).

Whether the Conqueror was responsible for bringing *Bob* to Britain, we can't be sure. But Roberts seem to have soon sprung up in the Anglo-Saxon world. Robert I (the Bruce) was the first king of Scotland in the fourteenth century, followed by his grandson, Robert II (the Steward), whose title morphed into the "Stewart/Stuart" dynastic name.

Robert Guiscard (ca. 1015–1085) was conqueror of southern Italy, and Robert of Courtenay was Latin emperor of Constantinople from 1218 to 1228.

Although Robert Morris of Pennsylvania and Robert Treat Paine of Massachusetts signed the Declaration of Independence, there has been no American president or vice president Robert. Only Robert M. La Follette (Progressive) and Robert Dole (Republican) have been major party presidential nominee Bobs. But fourteen other nations have enjoyed—or, in some cases, survived—presidents and/or prime ministers named Robert or Roberto—from Walpole, Britain's first prime minister, to the notorious Mugabe of Zimbabwe.

# six

# Witty and Wise

**I**t's permanent, for now.   *—announcing that his new name would be "Bobby"*

**Roberto Kelly,** 1964–
baseball player

**S**ome people I've encountered in various phases of my career seem more certain of everything than I am of anything.

**Robert Rubin,** 1938–
financier/U.S. Treasury secretary

**I**t's not very often you get to see the *Lone Ranger* and Toronto the same night.

> *—on the guest appearance by Clayton Moore (TV's Lone Ranger) at a Blue Jays game*

**Bobby Bragan,** 1917–
baseball player/manager

**M**y own belief is that a fool will always find banana skins.

**Robert Priest,** 1951–
writer

**T**he three major administrative problems on a campus are sex for the students, athletics for the alumni, and parking for the faculty.

**Robert M. Hutchins,** 1899–1977
president, University of
Chicago/editor

**B**urns' Hog-Weighing Method: (1) Get a perfectly symmetrical plank and balance it across a sawhorse. (2) Put the hog on one end of the plank. (3) Pile rocks on the other end until the plank is again perfectly balanced. (4) Carefully guess the weight of the rocks.

> **Robert Burns,** 1758–1796
> poet

**W**hen the Supreme Court moved to Washington in 1800, it was provided with no books, which probably accounts for the high quality of early opinions.

> **Robert H. Jackson,** 1892–1954
> U.S. attorney general/Supreme
> Court justice

**I** used to play golf with a guy who cheated so badly that he once had a hole in one and wrote down zero on the scorecard.

> **Bob Bruce,** 1933–
> baseball player

**I**f you watch a game, it's fun. If you play it, it's recreation. If you work at it, it's golf.

> **Bob Hope,** 1903–2003
> comedian

**A** passion, an obsession, a romance, a nice acquaintanceship with trees, sand, and water. *—on golf*

> **Bob Ryan,** 1946–
> journalist

**I** just think it's absolute nonsense to have individuals licensed to use assault weapons. Even if you're an avid hunter, my sense of fairness is, if you can't hit that target in three shots, you don't deserve to.

> **Robert Michel,** 1923–
> U.S. congressman, Illinois

**V**anity dies hard; in some obstinate cases it outlives the man.

**Robert Louis Stevenson,**
1850–1894
writer

**N**obody knows me like I knows me, and I knows me well.

**Robert Klein,** 1942–
comedian/writer

**T**o be born a gentleman is an accident, to die one is an achievement.

**Robert Goddard,** 1954–
writer

**I**'ve found that in the limbo dance of pettiness, I'm always able to go a little bit lower.　　　　　　　　　　—Way to Go, Smith

**Bob Smith,** 1958–
comedian/writer

**Y**es folks, their gold medal looks the same as everybody else's.

*—on Olympic rhythmic gymnastics competition*

> **Bob Costas,** 1952–
> sportscaster

**W**hen we made *Dumb and Dumber*, I was asked if I thought the movie would be offensive to dumb people. I didn't think it would, because I didn't think anyone would be willing to stand up and represent dumb people everywhere.

> **Bobby Farrelly,** 1958–
> filmmaker

**I** don't like country music, but I don't mean to denigrate those who do. And for the people who like country music, denigrate means "put down."

> **Bob Newhart,** 1929–
> comedian

**S**torytelling and copulation are the two chief forms of amusement in the South. They're inexpensive and easy to procure.

> **Robert Penn Warren,** 1905–1989
> writer

**O**nly two things I don't do. I don't ask people for money, and I don't judge a queen contest. There can't be more than one queen, and everybody else wants to burn your barn down.

> **Bob Evans,** 1918–
> founder, Bob Evans restaurant chain

**I** remember the IHOP that got turned into a Japanese restaurant . . . I found it quite interesting, but I never ordered the buttermilk sushi.

> **Bob Mould,** 1960–
> musician/songwriter

**T**his job is better than I could get if I used my college degree, which, at this point, I can't remember what it was in.

> **Bob Golic,** 1957–
> football player

**I**'ve never been out of this country, but I've been to California. Does that count?

> **Bob Bergland,** 1928–
> U.S. secretary of agriculture/ U.S.
> congressman, Minnesota

**P**eople say I am ruthless. I am not ruthless. And if I find the man who is calling me ruthless, I shall destroy him.

> **Robert F. Kennedy,** 1925–1968
> U.S. attorney general/U.S. senator,
> New York

**A** jury consists of twelve persons chosen to decide who has the better lawyer.

> **Robert Frost,** 1874–1963
> poet

**I** don't have lunches, dinners, go to plays or movies. I don't meditate, escalate, deviate, or have affairs. So I have plenty of time.

> **Robert A. Gottlieb,** 1931–
> editor

**N**ot if I had to have his brain too.

*—asked if he wanted Randy Myers's fastball*

> **Bob Ojeda,** 1957–
> baseball player

**I** had bad days on the field. But I didn't take them home with me. I left them in a bar along the way home.

> **Bob Lemon,** 1920–2000
> baseball player

**I**f prostate cancer was a fast-growing cancer I would not be here today, but because it is a slow-growing cancer, the doctors gave me estrogen for six months. My voice didn't get any higher, but my breasts were very sensitive.

> **Robert Goulet,** 1933–
> singer/actor

**I** know that you believe you understand what you think I said, but I'm not sure you realize that what you heard is not what I meant.

> **Robert McCloskey,** 1915–2003
> writer/illustrator

**W**ith a written agreement you have a prayer; with a verbal agreement you have nothing but air.

**Robert Ringer,** 1938–
writer

**I**'ve discovered that the less I say, the more rumors I start.

**Bobby Clarke,** 1949–
hockey player/manager

**H**e doesn't know the meaning of the word fear, but then again he doesn't know the meaning of most words.

**Bobby Bowden,** 1929–
football coach

**S**ilence is not only golden, it is seldom misquoted.

**Bob Monkhouse,** 1928–
comedian

**B**eing a philosopher, I have a problem for every solution.

> **Robert Zend,** 1929–1985
> writer

**B**e wary of strong drink. It can make you shoot at tax collectors . . . and miss.

> **Robert A. Heinlein,** 1907–1988
> writer

**W**ine is bottled poetry.

> **Robert Louis Stevenson,**
> 1850–1894
> writer

**I** know I'm drinking myself to a slow death, but then I'm in no hurry.

> **Robert Benchley,** 1889–1945
> humorist

**I** was graduated with "summa cum laude" in the eyes of the drinking fraternity, but not in the eyes of the dean.

**Robert Holbrook Smith, MD
(Dr. Bob),** 1879–1950
founder, Alcoholics Anonymous

**I**f people take the trouble to cook, you should take the trouble to eat.

**Robert Morley,** 1908–1992
actor

**T**rying to hit him was like trying to eat Jell-O with chopsticks. Once in a while you might get a piece, but most of the time you go hungry. *—on pitcher Phil Niekro*

**Bobby Murcer,** 1946–
baseball player

**V**egetarianism is harmless enough, though it is apt to fill a man with wind and self-righteousness.

> **Robert Hutchinson, MD,**
> 1871–1960
> president, Royal College of
> Physicians

**T**he last man in the world whose opinion I would take on what to eat would be a doctor. It is far safer to consult a waiter, and not a bit more expensive.

> **Robert Lynd,** 1879–1970
> sociologist

**N**othing more strongly arouses our disgust than cannibalism, yet we make the same impression on Buddhists and vegetarians, for we feed on babies, though not our own.

> **Robert Louis Stevenson,**
> 1850–94
> writer

**H**ealth food may be good for the conscience but Oreos taste a hell of a lot better.

> **Robert Redford,** 1937–
> actor/filmmaker

**A** big man is always accused of gluttony, whereas a wizened or osseous man can eat like a refugee at every meal, and no one ever notices his greed.

> **Robertson Davies,** 1913–1995
> writer

**O** Whiskey! Soul o' plays an' pranks!
Accept a Bardie's gratefu' thanks!
When wanting thee, what tuneless cranks
Are my poor verses!

—*"Scotch Drink"*

> **Robert Burns,** 1759–1796
> poet

**W**ho covets more is evermore a slave.

> **Robert Herrick,** 1591–1674
> poet

**I** like whiskey. I always did, and that is why I never drink it.

> **Robert E. Lee,** 1807–1870
> U.S. military leader/general in
> chief of the Confederacy

**M**usic is the wine that fills the cup of silence.

> **Robert Fripp,** 1946–
> musician/composer

**I**n the republic of mediocrity, genius is dangerous.

> **Robert Green Ingersoll,**
> 1833–1899
> lawyer/politician/orator

**S**ome facts are so simple that clever people can't accept them.

**Robert Locke,** 1932–
writer/scholar

**I**n our country are evangelists and zealots of many different political, economic, and religious persuasions whose fanatical conviction is that all thought is divinely classified into two kinds—that which is their own and that which is false and dangerous.

**Robert H. Jackson,** 1892–1954
U.S. attorney general/Supreme
Court justice

**T**here are two kinds of people, those who finish what they start and so on.

**Robert Byrne,** 1930–
writer/billiards authority

**T**here may be said to be two classes of people in the world: those who constantly divide the people of the world into two classes, and those who do not.

> **Robert Benchley,** 1889–1945
> humorist

**S**ay you were standing with one foot in the oven and one foot in an ice bucket. According to the percentage people, you would be perfectly comfortable.

> **Bobby Bragan,** 1917–
> baseball player

**I**f you let other people do it for you, they will do it to you.

> **Robert Anthony,** 1916–
> writer

**T**o know what you prefer, instead of humbly saying "Amen" to what the world tells you you ought to prefer, is to keep your soul alive.

> **Robert Louis Stevenson,**
> 1850–1894
> writer

**I**t is not easy to know what you like. Most people fool themselves their entire lives about this. Self-acquaintance is a rare condition.

> **Robert Henri,** 1865–1929
> artist

**A** civilization in which there is not a continuous controversy about important issues is on the way to totalitarianism and death.

> **Robert M. Hutchins,** 1899–1977
> president, University of
> Chicago/editor

**D**iscussion is an exchange of knowledge; an argument an exchange of ignorance.

**Robert Quillen,** 1887–1948
humorist

**N**ever argue; repeat your assertion.

**Robert Owen,** 1771–1858
businessman/social reformer

**P**eople don't ask for facts in making up their minds. They would rather have one good, soul-satisfying emotion than a dozen facts.

**Robert Keith Leavitt,** 1895–1967
writer/historian

**N**othing is more moving than beauty which is unaware of itself, except for ugliness which is.

**Robert Mallet,** 1810–1881
geologist

**B**y cultivating the beautiful we scatter the seeds of heavenly flowers, as by doing good we cultivate those that belong to humanity.

> **Robert A. Heinlein,** 1907–1988
> writer

**C**ulture takes away the simple human in us, but gives us more complex and sophisticated power.

> **Robert A. Johnson,** 1921–
> psychologist

**I**n nature there are neither rewards nor punishments; there are consequences.

> **Robert Green Ingersoll,**
> 1833–1899
> lawyer/politician/orator

**H**e might be a very clever man by nature for aught I know, but he laid so many books upon his head that his brains could not move.

> **Robert Hall,** 1764–1831
> clergyman

**B**ooks are good enough in their own way, but they are a poor substitute for life.

> **Robert Louis Stevenson,**
> 1850–1894
> writer

**L**earn to love good books. There are treasures in books that all the money of the world cannot buy, but that the poorest laborer in the world can have for nothing.

> **Robert Green Ingersoll,**
> 1833–1899
> lawyer/politician/orator

**Y**ou should allow your children a maximum of twenty to thirty minutes a day of television viewing. The rest of the time, you say, "If you don't read, you don't eat, make up your mind." What will it be like to live in a country where no one reads?

> **Robert Bly,** 1926–
> writer

**A** desire to be in charge of our own lives, a need for control, is born in each of us. It is essential to our mental health, and our success, that we take control.

> **Bob Bennett,** 1933–
> U.S. senator, Utah

**T**he quality of a university is measured more by the kind of student it turns out than the kind it takes in.

> **Robert J. Kibbee,** 1920–1982
> chancellor, City University of
> New York

**I**f you feel that you have both feet planted on level ground, then the university has failed you.

> **Robert Goheen,** 1919–
> president, Princeton
> University/diplomat

**E**ducation is not to reform students or amuse them or to make them expert technicians. It is to unsettle their minds, widen their horizons, inflame their intellects, teach them to think straight, if possible.

> **Robert M. Hutchins,** 1899–1977
> president, University of
> Chicago/editor

**I**gnorance gives a sort of eternity to prejudice, and perpetuity to error.

> **Robert Hall,** 1764–1831
> clergyman

**F**ullness of knowledge always means some understanding of the depths of our ignorance; and that is always conducive to humility and reverence.

**Robert Millikan,** 1953–

physicist

**L**et a student enter the school with this advice: No matter how good the school is, his education is in his own hands. All education must be self-education.

**Robert Henri,** 1865–1929

artist

**W**hen one teaches, two learn.

**Robert Half,** 1918–

businessman

It is a thousand times better to have common sense without education than to have education without common sense.

**Robert Green Ingersoll,**
1833–1899
lawyer/politician/orator

The open society, the unrestricted access to knowledge, the unplanned and uninhibited association of men for its furtherance—these are what may make a vast, complex, ever growing, ever changing, ever more specialized and expert technological world, nevertheless a world of human community.

**J. Robert Oppenheimer,**
1904–1967
physicist

If we wish to make a new world we have the material ready. The first one, too, was made out of chaos.

**Robert Quillen,** 1887–1948
humorist

**M**alady is another country, scary and strange. Its borderline is only one microbe, a rogue cell, an accident away.

**Robert Lipsyte,** 1938–
writer

**P**art of the intelligence of the human body is how quickly it forgets pain. It cannot be recalled no matter how hard you try or how much you pretend.

**Bob Kerrey,** 1943–
governor/U.S. senator, Nebraska/
president, New School University

**P**erfectionism is a dangerous state of mind in an imperfect world.

**Robert Hillyer,** 1895–1961
poet/educator

**M**any attempts to communicate are nullified by saying too much.

> **Robert Greenleaf,** 1904–1990
> management authority

**T**here are too many people and too few human beings.

> **Robert Zend,** 1929–1985
> writer

**T**hanksgiving comes to us out of the prehistoric dimness, universal to all ages and all faiths. At whatever straws we must grasp, there is always a time for gratitude and new beginnings.

> **J. Robert Moskin,** 1923–
> writer/editor

**L**ove God and trust your feelings.

> **Robert C. Pollock,** 1901–1978
> philosopher

**L**ive merrily as thou canst, for by honest mirth we cure many passions of the mind.

> **Robert Burton,** 1577–1640
> scholar/clergyman

**M**y creed is this:
Happiness is the only good.
The place to be happy is here.
The time to be happy is now.
The way to be happy is to make others so.

> **Robert Green Ingersoll,**
> 1833–1899
> lawyer/politician/orator

**T**he most important and the most unselfish thing you or I or anyone has to do in this world is to *take care of number one*!

> **Bob Cummings,** 1908–1990
> actor

**A**nyone can carry his burden, however hard, until nightfall. Anyone can do his work, however hard, for one day. Anyone can live sweetly, patiently, lovingly, purely, till the sun goes down. And this is all life really means.

**Robert Louis Stevenson,**
1850–1894
writer

**H**ow little do they see what is, who frame their hasty judgments upon that which seems.

**Robert Southey,** 1774–1843
poet

**T**he only Zen you can find on the tops of mountains is the Zen you bring up there.

**Robert M. Pirsig,** 1928–
philosopher

**I**f you look closely enough, amid the merciless and the bitter, there is always the chance that you may find comfort and the promise of something good.

> **Bob Greene,** 1947–
> journalist

**I**t is a simple but sometimes forgotten truth that the greatest enemy to present joy and high hopes is the cultivation of retrospective bitterness.

> **Robert G. Menzies,**
> 1894–1978
> prime minister, Australia

**T**he optimist thinks this is the best of all possible worlds. The pessimist fears it is true.

> **J. Robert Oppenheimer,**
> 1904–1967
> physicist

My friends know that to me happiness is when I am merely miserable and not suicidal.

**Bob Fosse,** 1927–1987
director/choreographer

If you listen to your fears, you will die never knowing what a great person you might have been.

**Robert H. Schuller,** 1926–
clergyman

Don't believe the world owes you a living; the world owes you nothing—it was here first.

**Robert Jones Burdette,**
1844–1914
clergyman/writer

**I**t's a sign of mediocrity when you express gratitude with moderation.

> **Roberto Benigni,** 1952–
> actor/filmmaker

**T**he unexamined life is not worth living.

> **Socrates,** ca. 470 BC–399 BC
> philosopher

**T**he examined life is no picnic.

> **Robert Fulghum,** 1937–
> writer/clergyman

**J**udgment comes from experience and great judgment comes from bad experience.

> **Bob Packwood,** 1932–
> U.S. senator, Oregon

**B**e Prepared.

*—scout motto*

> **Robert Baden-Powell,**
> 1857–1941
> soldier/writer/founder
> of the Boy Scouts

**I**f you get simple beauty and naught else, you get about the best thing God invents.

> **Robert Browning,** 1812–1889
> poet

**N**ever ignore a gut feeling, but never believe that it's enough.

> **Robert Heller,** 1933–
> editor/management authority

**A**rt is much less important than life, but what a poor life without it.

> **Robert Motherwell,** 1915–1991
>
> artist

**T**he poem . . . is a little myth of man's capacity of making life meaningful. And in the end, the poem is not a thing we see—it is, rather, a light by which we may see—and what we see is life.

> **Robert Penn Warren,** 1905–1989
>
> writer

# The Best of Bob

The Pulitzer Prize has been awarded to Bobs and Roberts forty times, including four to Robert Frost, four to Robert E. Sherwood, and three to Robert Penn Warren. Robert Lowell and Robert A. Caro each won twice. Although journalist Bob Woodward has never won, he was nominated—not for his famous reporting on Watergate, but for the later Iran-Contra affair. In 1973, the Pulitzer for the Watergate story went to his paper, the *Washington Post*.

Roberts were honored with the Nobel Prize on twenty-four occasions, with six wins each in chemistry, economics, and physics. Five Bobs have won for medicine, and the 1937 prize for peace was given to Britain's Robert Cecil, a principal architect of the League of Nations.

# seven

# A Bob for All Seasons

What Youth deemed crystal, Age finds out was dew.

—*"Jochanan Hakkadosh"*

**Robert Browning,** 1812–1889
poet

I don't feel old. I don't feel anything till noon. That's when it's time for my nap.

**Bob Hope,** 1903–2003
comedian

**E**ven at our birth, death does but stand aside a little. And every day he looks towards us and muses somewhat to himself whether that day or the next he will draw nigh.

**Robert Bolt,** 1924–1995
dramatist

**B**y the time a man is thirty-five he knows that the images of the right man, the tough man, the true man which he received in high school do not work in life.

**Robert Bly,** 1926–
writer

**F**or God's sake give me the young man who has brains enough to make a fool of himself!

**Robert Louis Stevenson,**
1850–1894
writer

**A** young man's ambition is to get along in the world and make a place for himself—half your life goes that way, till you're forty-five or fifty. Then, if you're lucky, you make terms with life, you get released.

**Robert Penn Warren,** 1905–1989
writer

**I** don't know what I look like to you but as far as I am concerned, I am a young, handsome chap holding forth, not some little old man in glasses with a bald head.

**Bob Hoskins,** 1942–
actor

**S**ee, what you're meant to do when you have a midlife crisis is buy a fast car, aren't you? Well, I've always had fast cars. It's not that. It's the fear that you're past your best. It's the fear that the stuff you've done in the past is your best work.

**Robbie Coltrane,** 1950–
actor

**N**o true artist ends with the style that he expected to have when he began, any more than anyone's life unrolls in the particular manner that one expected when young.

> **Robert Motherwell,** 1915–1991
> artist

**A**h. The clock is always slow;
It is later than you think.

*—"It Is Later Than You Think"*

> **Robert W. Service,** 1874–1958
> poet

**T**here is no distance on this earth as far away as yesterday.

—So Love Returns

> **Robert Nathan,** 1894–1985
> writer

**T**ime does not heal, it only accommodates.

> **Bob Geldof,** 1951–
> singer/songwriter/activist

**W**hy does everyone talk about the past? All that counts is tomorrow's game.

> **Roberto Clemente,** 1934–1972
> baseball player

**I**t's been a hell of a life and it's been an incredible ride. And when I die, whoever gets this seat better buckle up, 'cause it's a lotta ups and a lotta downs. But I wouldn't have it any other way.

> **Robert Blake,** 1933–
> actor

**Y**ou can't cheat death, but you can cheat life. By not living.

> **Robert Mapplethorpe,**
> 1946–1989
> photographer

**L**ive as long as you may, the first twenty years are the longest half of your life.

—*"The Doctor"*

> **Robert Southey,** 1774–1843
> poet

**W**hy die when you've just learned to live?

> **Bob Cummings,** 1908–1990
> actor

**R**emember the great adversity of art or anything else is a hurried life.

> **Robert James Waller,** 1939–
> writer

**M**y older son who is, I think, here tonight, is forty-one years old. Which is odd because so am I.

> **Robert Parker,** 1932–
> writer

**D**on't forget that at forty the reserve of a lifetime is not easily broken. It has been built up to protect the most sensitive spots.

**Robert Falcon Scott,** 1868–1912
British naval officer/South Pole
expedition leader

**I** never decide whether it's time to retire during training camp.

**Bob Christian,** 1968–
football player

**I** don't look back with any bitterness, though there are a couple of judgment calls and some '80s hairdos that I'd like to do over.

**Rob Lowe,** 1964–
actor

**I**'m just glad to be feeling better. I really thought I'd be seeing Elvis soon. —*after hospitalization in 1997*

**Bob Dylan,** 1941–
singer/songwriter

**M**ost poets are dead by their late twenties.

> **Robert Graves,** 1895–1985
> writer

**W**hen it comes to my own turn to lay my weapons down, I shall do so with thankfulness and fatigue, and whatever be my destiny afterward, I shall be glad to lie down with my fathers in honor. It is human at least, if not divine.

> **Robert Louis Stevenson,**
> 1850–1894
> writer

**G**ather ye rosebuds while ye may,
Old Time is still a-flying;
And this same flower that smiles today,
Tomorrow will be dying.

*—"To the Virgins, to Make Much of Time"*

> **Robert Herrick,** 1591–1674
> poet

**W**hat's a man's age? He must hurry more, that's all; Cram in a day, what his youth took a year to hold. *—"The Flight of the Duchess"*

**Robert Browning,** 1812–1889
poet

**I** won't lie. I tried to lie to a girl about my age. She started laughing right in my face and said, "I know more about you than you do." That's not good.

**Robert Evans,** 1930–
filmmaker

**S**o sweet love seemed that April morn,
When first we kissed beside the thorn,
So strangely sweet, it was not strange
We thought that love could never change.

*—"So Sweet Love Seemed That April Morn"*

**Robert Bridges,** 1844–1930
poet

The secret to a happy life is to run out of cash and air at the same time.

**Bobby Layne,** 1926–1986
football player

Time marches on. And eventually you realize it's marching across your face.

—Steel Magnolias

**Robert Harling,** 1951–
screenwriter

We advance in years somewhat in the manner of an invading army in a barren land; the age that we have reached, as the saying goes, we but hold with an outpost, and still keep open communications with the extreme rear and first beginnings of the march.

—Virginibus Puerisque and Other Papers

**Robert Louis Stevenson,**
1850–1894
writer

**D**eath ends a life, not a relationship.

> **Robert Benchley,** 1889–1945
> humorist

**N**o matter what you've accomplished in life, the size of your funeral will depend largely on the weather.

> **Bob Devaney,** 1915–1997
> football coach

# Believe-Bob-or-Not

**R**obert Pershing Wadlow, born in Alton, Illinois, in 1918, reigns as the tallest man in recorded medical history. He measured eight feet eleven inches just before his untimely death at age twenty-two.

Bob "the Vaulting Vicar" Richards was a minister and two-time Olympic gold medal–winning pole-vaulter. He was also the first athlete to be pictured on the front of a box of Wheaties.

By the age of thirty-three, British explorer Robert Swan had become the first man to walk to both the South (1985) and the North (1989) Poles.

Robert Parish, the oldest man ever to play in the National Basketball Association, was nearly forty-four when he retired in 1977. Parish was a nine-time nominee to the NBA All-Star team.

Minnesota is the "Land of 10,000 Lakes," and the land of about 1,000 Bob Johnsons, unique men who share the most popular name in the state.

# INDEX